Harry Leverett Nelson

Bird-Songs about Worcester

Harry Leverett Nelson

Bird-Songs about Worcester

ISBN/EAN: 9783337107307

Printed in Europe, USA, Canada, Australia, Japan

Cover: Foto ©ninafisch / pixelio.de

More available books at **www.hansebooks.com**

BIRD-SONGS

ABOUT

WORCESTER.

BY

HARRY LEVERETT NELSON, A. M.

BOSTON
LITTLE, BROWN, AND COMPANY
1889

The time of the singing of birds is come.

*I rose anon, and thoght I wolde goon
Into the wode, to here the briddes singe,
When that the mysty vapour was agoon,
And clere and feyer was the morownyng.*

. . . . .

*And in I went to here the briddes songe,
Which on the braunches, bothe in pleyn and vale,
So loude songe that al the wode ronge.*

INTRODUCTION.

THE letters here collected were first published in Worcester newspapers. The theme, almost universally attractive, has found few students willing to devote to it that degree of patient observation and comparison necessary to its knowledge. That the birds are singing about us, that their music forms part of the great harmony of Nature, that when noblest desires and sweetest anticipations inspire our courage, then are our cheerful spirits most nearly in tune with the songs of these unfeed minstrels, — all this we know.

But there is an added delight, which they who seek it find, in intimate acquaintance with the singer, in possessing personal information of the place and hour of his concert, in listening for his vernal overture, and appreciating the brightening blessing of his season's farewell.

"Come, hear this woman, she sings like a nightingale." "But I can hear the nightingale." Not altogether wise in the philosopher to reject the one, but how can we excuse neglect of the other?

In the rural city where the writer of the letters lived, it came to many as a matter of surprise that there was so much to study, so ample a source of gratification in the birds about us. Filled as they are with the enthusiasm of the true lover, the letters served as a guide for others to pleasures not before revealed.

On the sixteenth of August, eighteen hundred and eighty-nine, HARRY LEVERETT NELSON, then hardly past the portals of his professional career, was quietly turned aside into that silent path which leads we know not whither. Reflections such as have here been imperfectly expressed, persuaded several of his friends that his letters in more permanent form would be welcomed by former readers and find appreciation in wider circles. In this belief we present them just as they came from his pen, with but the corrections of a careful proof-reader. We have added a letter on another topic, which seemed to us of interest.

R. H.
C. F. A.
C. M. R.

WORCESTER, MASS.,
    November, 1889.

CONTENTS.

LETTER		PAGE
I.	APRIL BIRDS	9
II.	APRIL BIRDS (*Continued*)	20
III.	APRIL BIRDS (*Concluded*)	31
IV.	MAY BIRDS	43
V.	MAY BIRDS (*Continued*)	55
VI.	JUNE BIRDS	67
VII.	MIDSUMMER SONGSTERS	79
VIII.	BIRD NOMENCLATURE. — SOME ENGLISH AND AMERICAN BIRDS	90
IX.	THE BIRDS OF PRINCETON	100
X.	OFF CAPE COD. — WHALING IN MASSACHUSETTS BAY	113

Bird-Songs about Worcester.

I.

APRIL BIRDS.

WORCESTER, April 9, 1887.

MY DEAR MR. EDITOR, — In contributing this series of letters to your esteemed paper I am realizing an idea I have long had in mind of attempting through your columns to awaken some general interest in the study of bird songs. In pursuance of this idea I shall endeavor in this letter to describe the songs of some of our earliest birds, which it will be comparatively easy to master thus early in the season, before the arrival of the countless hosts of others, which will soon make their appearance from the South. I trust, also, that I shall be able to facilitate this study by the method I shall adopt of describing actual walks about Worcester, and of referring continually to well-known and accessible localities.

Yesterday was a cloudless April day, and the sun tempered the chilliness in the air caused by the snow-banks along the roadside. As I walked up Highland Street by Mr. Salisbury's house, my ears were at once saluted by the pretty trills of the song-sparrow (*melospiza melodia*) issuing from the orchard and fields west of the house. At this season this beautiful singer cannot be mistaken, uttering three or four pipes, or whistles, followed by canary-like trills and quavers, not very loud, but spirited and vivacious. There is, perhaps, no other of our birds whose song varies so much in detail and execution, though the quality and theme are always the same, and sometimes the same singer will give us five or six different variations in rapid succession without changing his perch. The little vesper-sparrow (*poocætes gramineus*), which will now soon be with us, pours forth a song so similar to some of these variations that it requires considerable practice and study to distinguish them with certainty. Until the robins are in song, this modest little song-sparrow, in his plain brown suit, furnishes nine-tenths of our bird music. Proceeding up Highland Street I am greeted with its song from all parts of Elm Park. This bird has been with us now for three or four weeks, and, like the blue-bird, has been filling the bleak, barren fields with its music since its first appearance.

All the way up the street the much-abused English sparrows kept up a constant chatter to the south towards the city, while to the north, especially among the evergreens opposite the Merrifield estate, the slate-colored snow-birds (*junco hyemalis*) were everywhere to be seen. These snow-birds, with their ashy-black backs, white bellies, and white lateral tail-feathers opening and shutting like a fan as they fly before you, are for the first few weeks in April more numerous than the individuals of all other species combined. Although, as their name implies, they occasionally stay with us through the winter months, they are much more abundant in the early spring and late fall. By the first of May they will nearly all have left for the White Mountains and the North, where they pass the summer. I have, however, seen a few pairs near the summit of Mount Wachusett in the summer, and have no doubt that they breed there. Numerous as are the snow-birds, they contribute but little to our spring music, their only song being an occasional low jingle, not, however, unpleasing to the ear. In the Park I found these birds unusually abundant.[1]

[1] Nuttall says that the song of the snow-bird is "a few sweet, clear, and tender notes, almost similar to the touching warble of the European robin red-breast." It is among the finer and more delicate forecastings of earliest spring. — EDS.

As I stand in the road opposite Elm Park, I hear first, away off toward Sunnyside, and then from the slopes of Newton Hill, the soft, homesick warble of the bluebird (*sialia sialis*). It is impossible not to recognize the half-pathetic, tremulous note, so different from the cheerful ditty of the song-sparrow, with which it most frequently blends during the frosty days of March and April. The bluebird has been with us nearly a month, and is already pairing and beginning preparations for setting up housekeeping in some martin-box before the door, or in some deserted woodpecker's hole in the woods or fields.

On the morning of the 31st of March, walking along Pleasant Street, west of Newton Hill, I was surprised to hear from the snow-covered meadow below the piercing, long-drawn-out whistle of the meadowlark (*sturnella magna*). It is a veritable spring sound, fresh and strong, cleaving the frosty air like a knife. It is simple as the curve in form, beginning low, ascending and strengthening, and then descending. The larks may always be heard a little later in the season in the fields by Salisbury's Pond, east of the boulevard, and in the fields south and east of the Technical School, and I have even heard them on West street, in the neighborhood of the tennis-courts. This is one of our handsomest native birds, with his conspicuous yellow breast and martial bearing, and may be easily recognized by his peculiar hovering flight, not unlike the soaring of the hawk, and by his white tail-feathers.

The robins (*turdus migratorius*) have been with us in abundance for two weeks, but though I heard them yesterday on all sides screaming and calling, none were yet in song. The spring carnival had not yet begun. For the rest of the month, however, these thrushes will be musical enough. April is, *par excellence*, the robins' month. The wood-thrush and veery wait for May; but what is sweeter and more inspiring than the strong, profuse song of the robin which he carols forth for an hour at a time in the April twilight from some leafless tree in the pasture or orchard?

Since writing the above, on the evening of the date of this letter, I have heard robins in full song all along Harvard Street, and they have now, undoubtedly, generally begun singing in all parts of the city:

Another bird, which comes in April, or even in March, is the phœbe-bird (*sayornis fuscus*), the pioneer of the fly-catchers. Its cheerful and rapidly repeated *phee-bee, phee-bee, phee-bee* is its spring note. In the summer we hear *phe-ee-bee, phe-ee-bee*, slower, sadder, and more in accordance with the advancing season.

The common chickadee, or black-capped titmouse (*parus atricapillus*), has, in addition to its ordinary *dee-dee-dee*, a spring note so much like the later note of the phœbe that they cannot easily be distinguished. I have never seen the pretty note of the chickadee mentioned in any book but Thoreau's "Early Spring in Massachusetts," edited by Mr. H. G. O. Blake. I first heard it myself on a bright, sunny day, toward the end of February, on Kendall Street. The chickadee is one of our very few birds that stay with us all the year round, and it is also one of the few birds that have inspired the native muse. Mr. Emerson's "Titmouse" ranks with his "Humble-bee" among the most popular and well-known of his poems.

Yesterday I saw a pair of white-bellied nuthatches (*sitta carolinensis*) in an orchard near Kendall Street, and heard their harsh, rasping *qua-qua-qua*, which it is quite impossible to mistake. Last fall they were abundant all through the neighborhood, and were very conspicuous with their glistening dark-blue backs and heads, white breasts, and queer, short tails. Like the chickadee, the nuthatch lives on the larvæ in the bark, and he is our only bird that hangs head downward as he creeps around the trunk in his search for food. The nuthatch breeds far north of us, whither he will soon be hastening.[1]

The pigeon woodpecker, or high-hole, or flicker (*colaptes auratus*), is a characteristic April bird, which, unlike the nuthatch, comes to tarry, and though I have as yet missed his long, loud *if-if-if-if*, reminding one somewhat of the scream of the robin, yet it will soon be heard re-echoing through the outskirts of the city. Though a handsome, jaunty fellow, he is much fonder of being heard than seen, which seems all the stranger, as his voice is far from pleasing or musical.

The blue grackle, or crow-blackbird (*quiscalus versicolor*) is already abundant in the Rural Cemetery, one of his favorite haunts, and it is amusing indeed to watch him lift his wings and jerk up his tail in his desperate efforts to sing, all resulting in the most pitiful wheezing and sputtering,— the mere parody of a musical performance.

[1] The white-bellied nuthatch sometimes breeds in Massachusetts. — EDS.

The loud *conqueree* of the red-shouldered blackbird (*agelaius phœniceus*) is already heard among the marshes of North Pond, and the long, sliding, monotonous chant of the common little chipping-sparrow (*spizella socialis*) I have suspected that I heard once or twice from our orchard, but the real flight of this species, it is clear, is hardly yet begun.

Within the next week or two the purple-finch and the goldfinch, the vesper-sparrow and the field-sparrow will have put in an appearance; but with these exceptions there will be few prominent arrivals before the first of May. Not till then, at the earliest, may we expect the brown-thrush and the cat-bird, the wood-thrush and the veery, the orioles and the bobolinks, the vireos, and the host of warblers that come by the first of June.

I would say in conclusion to this letter that any of your readers who may be interested in the subject of birds and their singing will find the first chapter of John Burroughs' "Wake Robin," and the chapter in Bradford Torrey's "Birds in the Bush" entitled "A Bird Lover's April," delightful and profitable reading regarding our early birds. I must not omit to mention also a book I have already referred to, Thoreau's "Early Spring in Massachusetts," comprising extracts from his journal, which, however, brings down the season only to about the eighth of April. ·

II.

APRIL BIRDS (Continued).

WORCESTER, April 19, 1887.

MY DEAR MR. EDITOR, — Since my last letter the vesper, field, and chipping sparrows, the purple-finch, goldfinch, and blue-backed swallows have made their appearance from the South, the robins have been singing everywhere, the pigeon-woodpecker has begun to shout, and the snow-birds have been growing fewer daily. The recent unseasonable weather, and yesterday's heavy snow-storm, have probably checked somewhat the onward tide of migration; but this is only temporary, and the season's steady advance is but little retarded. As most of our early birds are finches or sparrows, which live on the seeds of plants and weeds, they have been put to little inconvenience by the weather, for, so long as their food supply is ample, it is well known that with their warm clothing and highly organized systems, the birds are insensible to the extreme cold.

The most conspicuous arrival of the last few days is the vesper-sparrow, or bay-winged bunting, or grass-finch (*poocætes gramineus*). Up to the fifteenth of the month, of all his tribe, the song-sparrow had reigned supreme, but during the night of the fourteenth (for it is now well established that birds make their migrations in the night-time) there was a great flight of baywings. On the morning of the fifteenth, in the orchard north of Highland Street, just beyond Elm Park, I saw a flock of fifty or a hundred; and numerous individuals were singing freely, both in the orchard and all along the side of Newton Hill opposite. They are much more abundant now than they will be later in the season, as the great body will proceed farther north, leaving behind only a small fraction of their number to spend the summer with us here in Massachusetts. The song of this species is strikingly like the song sparrow's, but the voice is not so loud and ringing, and the two or three opening notes are less sharply emphasized. In general the difference between the two songs may be well expressed by saying that the one is more declamatory, the other more *cantabile*,— a difference such as might have been expected, considering the nervous, impetuous disposition of the song-sparrow and the placidity of the baywing. The sparrow may be easily identified by its size, which is considerably larger than that of the song-sparrow, and by the two white lateral quills of his tail, — less conspicuous, however, than in the snow bird, since there we have white against black, while here we have white against brown. John Burroughs finds in this little vesper-sparrow one of his favorite birds. Of him he says: "Not in meadows or orchards, but in high, breezy pasture-grounds will you look for him. His song is most noticeable after sundown, when other birds are silent, for which reason he has been aptly called the vesper-sparrow. Two or three long silver notes of rest and peace, ending in some subdued thrills or quavers, constitute each separate song. Such unambitious, unconscious melody! It is one of the most characteristic sounds in nature. The grass, the stones, the stubble, the furrow, the quiet herds and the warm twilight among the hills, are all subtilely expressed in this song; this is what they are at least capable of."

All along the ridge of hills on Burncoat Street, from Adams Square to the Summit, these birds are unusually abundant all through the season.

The field-sparrow, or bush-sparrow (*spizella pusilla*), though closely allied to the familiar chipping-sparrow, whom he strongly resembles in size and general appearance, is usually found remote from the abodes of man, either on the edge of the woods or in the waste pasture-lot overgrown with under-brush. His song is simplicity itself, consisting of two or three introductory whistles, followed by a whistle long and vibrating, but without trills or other embellishments. I often hear it near the border of the woods on the southwest slope of Millstone Hill, towards the city, and on the bushy hillside beyond Sunnyside, east of Peat Meadow. The field-sparrow enjoys the distinction of singing all summer long, even during the heat of the dog-days, long after most other birds have become silent. This bird I have heard once or twice this spring, though as yet it has hardly become abundant.

Of all the members of the sparrow family that stay with us to breed, the purple finch, or linnet (*carpodacus purpureus*), is the finest musician. Only the adult male is purple, however, and even he, according to Burroughs, looks as if he had been dipped in pokeberry juice and taken out before the dyeing process was half finished. The female and the young male are clad in plain brown. This finch appears in the spring, just when the elm-trees are beginning to leaf out, and he is supposed to feed on the bursting buds, to the no great benefit, I fancy, of the tree. I have not yet heard him about Worcester, but, spending last Sunday in Uxbridge, where the season is much more advanced than here, I was awakened early in the morning by his loud, warbling song proceeding from the old elm-tree in front of the farm-house.

The long, piercing note of the lark, arising from the meadows along the river, contrasted strangely with the song of the linnet, the two producing a curious and rather unusual medley.

The purple finch has a wonderfully sweet and protracted warble, the notes following one another with surprising rapidity, surpassing in this respect, Burroughs says, the music of almost any other bird. There is a strong resemblance to the song of the warbling vireo, and it was undoubtedly this finch which Thoreau tells us in his journal he heard in April, and was unable to identify, but would have judged to be the warbling vireo had it not been much too early in the season for the arrival of this bird. With the exception of the robin and the chipping-sparrow, the purple finch is the earliest of the birds that are equally common in the country and along the city streets. Last season I heard him early in April in one of the elms on Belmont Street, in front of the schoolhouse, and some weeks afterwards was surprised to find him singing in a maple-tree on Chestnut Street. This bird is an excellent example of the unequal distribution of certain species of birds through different parts of the country. He was formerly rare about Worcester, but of late years has become pretty abundant, while in some parts of the State he is almost never seen. About Cambridge both the purple finch and the house wren are said to be very abundant. About Worcester the wren is extremely rare.

On the afternoon of Easter Sunday, while walking on West Street, I heard a goldfinch in full song. The American goldfinch (*chrysomitris tristis*), when in full spring plumage, is one of the handsomest of our birds, with his bright yellow body and jet black wings. This bird and the yellow warbler are indiscriminately called "yellow birds," though the name seems more appropriate to the warbler, which is yellow all over. The goldfinch, however, is much the finer singer, belonging to the same family as the canary and our own sweet singing-sparrows. The song, twitter, and call-note of this finch are wonderfully like the canary's, and as a whole flock will often sing in chorus, you may get some conception of the effect of such a concert if you will imagine fifty canaries thus engaged out of doors. The goldfinch, like the purple finch, may almost be called a city bird, as he is often seen about our lawns and gardens. He is, however, especially fond of evergreen trees, and in the Rural Cemetery, where these trees abound, he is very abundant. The goldfinch sometimes remains with us in sheltered places through the winter, when he loses his brilliant plumage and takes on a sort of dull-green, neutral tint.

One of the commonest and, before the advent of the English sparrow, perhaps the most familiar and sociable of our birds, is the little chipping-sparrow (*spizella socialis*), with his russet-colored crown and plain ashy-gray breast. Only the scouts of the great body have as yet arrived, but within a very few days now every garden in the city will resound with the long sliding chant. Bradford Torrey, speaking of the song of this bird, says: "Who that knows it does not love his earnest, long-drawn trill, dry and tuneless as it is? I can speak for one, at all events, and he always has an ear open for it by the middle of April. It is the voice of a friend, — a friend so true and gentle and confiding that we do not care to ask whether his voice be smooth and his speech eloquent."

Some writers have compared the song of this sparrow to the clicking sound produced by the rapid and repeated striking together of two pebbles. This little bird, according to Wilson Flagg, is always the first performer in the early morning concert, trilling his humble song while it is still dark, even before the robins are yet awake; and though I am unable to corroborate this by personal experience, I do remember hearing its song last June from a cherry-tree in our garden at ten o'clock at night.

In the first flush of my ornithological studies I remember how long it took me to associate this simple little song, which I heard everywhere, in city and country alike, with the chipping-sparrow. At that time I had never seen it mentioned in the books, and I was long convinced that it must belong to some rare warbler which had suddenly become abundant in this vicinity. My experience in regard to this bird, and many others as well, would lead me to advise all other students of bird-songs to hesitate long before attributing a new and unknown song to any of our rarer and accidental birds. Very few such birds will be heard in an entire season.

When at Uxbridge, Sunday, while listening to the song of the purple finch, I saw a pair of white-bellied swallows (*tachycineta bicolor*) flying far over my head in the blue sky. This swallow is the first of his family to make his appearance in the spring, and after the purple martin, rare about Worcester, is the handsomest swallow we have. It is not, however, nearly so common here as the barn-swallow, being much more abundant on the sea-coast and in the neighborhood of large lakes. Before the white man came here the swallow built its nests in hollow trunks of trees, and still does so in unsettled parts of the country, but in this vicinity it generally nests in martin-boxes prepared for its reception.

III.

APRIL BIRDS (Concluded).

WORCESTER, April 30, 1887.

DEAR MR. EDITOR, — All day Thursday there had been a warm April rain, and yesterday morning it cleared up warm and clear, with hardly a breath of air to stir the half-unfolded leaves which glistened in the bright sunlight. All the conditions were favorable to bird-music, and I felt sure that a short walk into the country would not be unrewarded. Most of our birds, as is well known, sing more freely in the early morning and evening twilight, but more especially in the morning, when everything is fresh and green, and the whole face of nature seems to smile, suffused with the rays of the rising sun. On rainy days the birds will often sing all day long, and then their morning and vesper hymns receive less attention. But the best time of all to hear bird-songs is after a storm, when the clouds have cleared away and the sun shines bright again. Then the pent-up feelings of our feathered songsters find expression in the choicest and most ecstatic melody. Windy days are not so favorable to the study of bird-songs, and, generally speaking, the birds sing much more freely in warm weather that in cold.

Yesterday my walk took me out Lincoln Street to the little strip of woods west of Adams Square, — a favorite haunt of mine, and one of the best and most accessible regions in this vicinity for bird-music. As I had expected, I found all the birds in full song, — robins, pigeon-woodpeckers, bluebirds, song, vesper, field, and chipping sparrows. The vesper and field sparrows were unusually abundant and musical, and there had evidently been a flight of the latter species within a few days, as the edge of the woods was full of them. I doubt if I ever heard a more magnificent and varied concert of sparrow-music than on this occasion, — the lively ditty of the song-sparrow, the sweet, melodious trill of the vesper, the long, ringing whistle of the field-sparrow, and even the sliding jingle of the chipper. All contributed their part. There seemed nothing more to be desired, but a pleasure unexpected was still in store for me. Suddenly from the moist meadow at the foot of the hill there was wafted up to me what seemed a new sparrow-song, sweeter and more liquid than any I had ever heard. This was repeated again and again, and slowly it dawned upon me that I had heard this beautiful song before. More than six years ago, in the backwoods of Maine, on the shores of the Rangeley Lakes, I had become familiar with the sweet strain of the peabody bird, the white-throated sparrow, "the nightingale of the North," (*zonotrichia albicollis*); and now right here in Worcester, almost within the city limits, I heard his song blending with the music of our own familiar sparrows. I have forborne to mention in these letters the fox-colored sparrows, the winter wrens, the kinglets, the white-crowned sparrows, and other birds of the far North, many of whom are most accomplished songsters, but whose stay with us in the spring, during their migrations, is so brief that their music attracts little notice. But the peabody bird has a claim on me which I may not and would not dispute, — that of an old friend whose melody I knew and loved long before I took any special interest in bird-songs, and who is inseparably associated in my mind with sweet-scented primeval forests, with wild mountain trout-streams, and the weird screaming of the loon. The song of the peabody bird begins with a long, clear, wavering whistle, followed by two or three bars, *peabody, peabody, peabody,* of almost unequalled sweetness. John Burroughs, who had heard the bird in the Adirondacks, referring to the abrupt termination of its song, says: "If it could give us the finishing strains, of which this seems only the prelude, it would stand first among feathered songsters." In the White Mountains this song and that of the hermit-thrush are much admired by the summer pilgrim, and they are even mentioned in the guide-books among the other attractions of the region. How few that have been charmed with the music of these birds in their native wilds are aware that for a brief period every spring they pour forth the same melody almost at our very doorsteps! It is now generally admitted that all birds sing, more or less fitfully, during the spring migration, and it has lately been one of my most cherished dreams to hear the hermit-thrush (*turdus pallasii*) here at home in my own woods. I have already seen him this spring flitting through the woods like a ghost, silent and songless. In a few days, like the white-throated sparrow, he will have moved on in his journey to the North, and several seasons may be necessary before my hopes are realized.

While listening to the peabody bird, I am greeted by the humble trill of the pine-creeping warbler (*dendroica pinus*) singing in a hemlock-tree over my head. Foolish bird! His is a pretty song by itself, but beside the delicious sparrow music with which I am regaled, his feeble *tweet, weet, weet* sounds pitifully weak and unsatisfactory. This little warbler, however, is doubly welcome, both for his own sake and for the sake of the gorgeous company of which he is the forerunner. Our warblers are the daintiest, the most delicate and the most gaily attired of all our birds. In outward show, compared with these elegant little creatures, the plainly-dressed sparrows and thrushes are homely and unattractive enough. But with birds as with human beings, the law of compensation is inexorable, and we find the American warblers possessed of very inferior musical gifts. How different in Europe! Enough is said when I mention the nightingale as the most prominent representative of the family. Not only are the warblers feeble singers, but they are also most of them very difficult to identify, as they flit about in the dense foliage of the tree-tops in their search for their insect food. As we walk through the thick woods, we are generally conscious of a half-suppressed, insect-like music in the trees far over our heads, but seldom associate it with these gaudily-dressed visitors from the tropics. Some of the members of this family, however, like the oven-bird and the Maryland yellow-throats, are ground-warblers, and are much better known than most of their brethren, while the half-domesticated little yellow warbler is almost as familiar as the robin or the chipping-sparrow. The pine-creeping is the only warbler I have seen this season, but by the tenth of May probably he will be reinforced by the great body of his congeners. Of the forty varieties of warblers assigned by Audubon to North America only a dozen or more are ever seen in this vicinity, and many of these only twice a year, in the migrations, when on their way to or from British America. There are few greater contrasts in nature than that presented by these Northern warblers, many of them the most elegant of their family, seeking out the vast uninhabited forests of the far North in which to breed and rear their young.

As I walk along the edge of the woods my attention is attracted by a very noticeable tri-colored bird, nearly as large as a robin, flitting about in a heap of brush. The unmistakable piedness of his dress, and a sharp *cherawink* at once serve to identify him as the chewink, or towee-bunting, or ground-robin (*pipilo erythrophthalmus*). I had been expecting him for a day or two, as he always makes his appearance a little before May-day. Who but an ornithologist would suppose the bird to be a sparrow, with his glossy black back, bright chestnut breast, and clear white beneath, so totally unlike the plainly dressed members of that family with which we are familiar? Yet some resemblance in anatomical structure has settled the question in the scientific world; and a sparrow he shall be. Besides his *cherawink*, which is his alarm note, the bird has a rather musical call note, *tow-hee*, sometimes ending in a long sparrow-like trill, which perhaps sufficiently vindicates the ornithologists in their classification of him. The chewink is usually found, like the field-sparrow, in bushy pasture-lots or on the borders of the woods, and, like the sparrow, continues singing far into the summer. While picnicking at the Lake last August in the pine grove just above the Poor-Farm Bridge on the Shrewsbury side, I remember hearing the field-sparrows and chewinks singing in unison, while not another bird-note was to be heard in any direction.

On the tip top of a tree near by I espy a cow blackbird, or cow-bird (*molothrus pecoris*), emitting with commendable assiduity his queer, sibilant *cluck-see*. This bird has been with us a month, and should, perhaps, have been alluded to in one of my former letters. The male is glossy black, with the exception of the head, which is dark brown, and the female is brown all over. The cow-bird, as his name implies, is most abundant in the fields and pastures among the grazing herds of cattle. But the most remarkable thing about this bird is that it builds no nest of its own, but deposits its eggs surreptitiously in other birds' nests. This habit it shares exclusively, among all the birds known to science, with the European cuckoo, a bird with which, however, it is no wise allied. Ornithologists have speculated as to the explanation of this eccentricity exhibited by these widely different birds, but apparently in vain.

Dr. Coues suggests that perhaps sometime in the remote past some female cowbird, dilatory about the building of her nest, hit upon this easy expedient as a necessary makeshift, and that gradually the obnoxious custom extended to the whole tribe of cow-birds. The smaller birds are generally the victims, especially the chipping-sparrow, Maryland yellow-throat, and yellow-warbler. Generally the strange egg is hatched by the foster parents, and the young cow-bird is tended with all the solicitude bestowed on the rightful occupants of the nest. Sometimes, however, the birds thus imposed upon abandon their nest altogether, especially if it contains no eggs of their own, and occasionally they construct a two-story nest, leaving the cow-bird's egg in the basement. The thing that has always struck me as most remarkable about the cow-birds, though I have never seen it mentioned in the books, is the wonderful instinct that brings together into one flock of their kindred these young fledglings, all reared in different nests, by all sorts of foster-parents.

Walking deeper into the woods to gather a bunch of the beautiful blood-root flower (*sanguinaria canadensis*) which I find in full bloom, my attention is arrested by the loud hammering of the downy woodpecker (*picus pubescens*). It is astonishing how this little woodpecker, scarcely larger than a sparrow, makes the woods reverberate. He is one of our few birds that seem to be entirely destitute of all vocal expression, and it is perhaps only right, therefore, that Downy should be allowed to hammer away on his tree as noisily as he pleases. The downy woodpecker, like the chickadee, stays with us all the year round, and like the chickadee lives on the larvæ in the bark, which he has no difficulty in procuring at all seasons.

I had hoped yesterday to hear in these woods a brown-thrush, or at least a catbird, and had thought it just possible that some adventurous wood-thrush might have already arrived in summer quarters; but in this I was destined to disappointment. I had heard, however, the song of the peabody bird during his migration, and would not have exchanged it even for the wood-thrush's evening hymn.

IV.

MAY BIRDS.

WORCESTER, May 13, 1887.

MY DEAR MR. EDITOR, — The morning of May-day was bright and spring-like, and should have been signalized, it seemed to me, by the advent of a goodly number of birds, but not a single new song rewarded my usual Sunday walk. The next morning, however, I saw my first brown-thrush flitting about in the thickets by the side of the boulevard west of Elm Park, and he soon broke forth into the old familiar song. Wednesday morning was celebrated by the appearance of the first orioles, yellow-warblers, redstarts, black-and-white creeping-warblers, and least fly-catchers, and on Thursday evening I heard my first wood-thrush, which, with the possible exception of the orioles and Wilson's thrushes, was the most important arrival of the week. The Wilsons came Friday, and on Saturday and Sunday I heard my first cat-bird, warbling vireo, oven-bird, wood-pewee, and night-hawk.

The brown-thrush (*harporhynchus rufus*) and the cat-bird (*mimus carolinensis*) are thrushes belonging to the same genus with the mocking-bird, and, like this celebrated Southern songster, they have for a song a curious medley, which often suggests the notes of other birds. Ornithologists are now generally agreed, however, that this is really a song of their own, and that they are in no wise guilty of plagiarism. There is a very strong family likeness between their songs, and it is sometimes very difficult to distinguish them with certainty. The brown-thrush's *contralto*, however, is much fuller and rounder than the cat-bird's *soprano*, and he wants the cat-bird's feline mew, which has given this bird his name. The strong, clear *sow-wheat* of the brown-thrush, from which he has received in some quarters the name of the "planting-bird," is much less marked in the song of the cat-bird. On the whole, the thrasher must be judged to be much the finer singer, though the cat-bird's song is much sweeter than is generally supposed. The brown-thrush, the largest of all the thrushes, is a very conspicuous, long-tailed bird, with bright reddish-brown plumage, but is much less neighborly than the cat-bird, generally preferring the more retired woods and pastures. This bird is now in his glory, and it is almost impossible to go out into the country without hearing him on every side. In a little more than a month he will have become silent. Of the song of this bird Bradford Torrey writes: "His song is a grand improvisation. Such power and range of voice; such startling transitions; such endless variety; and withal such boundless enthusiasm and almost incredible endurance!"

Nearly allied to the brown-thrush, though of a different genus, are the wood-thrush, or song-thrush (*turdus mustelinus*) and the Wilson's thrush, or veery (*turdus fuscescens*), the most beautiful singers to be found in this vicinity. The wood-thrush may always be heard at this season in the early morning and evening, and in cloudy weather through the day, in Paine's Woods, in the neighborhood of the hermitage, while the veery is to be heard higher up on Millstone Hill, near the quarries. Both birds sing in the thick woods south of Hope Cemetery, and I often hear the wood-thrush in the woods west of Adams Square. The wood-thrush will continue singing nearly into August, but the veeries will become songless by the first of July. The song of the wood-thrush it is almost impossible to represent in words, but it is hard to mistake the bell-like purity of its voice, which cannot be confounded with the song of any other bird. In elaborate *technique* and delicious *portamento* it surpasses all the other thrushes. A peculiarly liquid *air-o-ee* is very beautiful, and a silvery jingle is often interspersed, so different from the rest of the song that it seems to the listener to proceed from some other bird. The wood-thrushes, more than any other birds I know of, exhibit various degrees of excellence, some individuals singing much more beautifully than others. The song of this bird is, perhaps, more likely than that of any other to attract the notice of the uninitiated, and is usually set down by such as a most remarkable and noteworthy phenomenon, though the wood-thrushes are really among the most abundant of our birds.

The song of the Wilson's thrush, or veery, is beautiful for its very simplicity, and of all birds' songs may most truly be called spiritual. It consists of a repetition of the words *ve-ee-ry, ve-ee-ry, ve-ee-ry*, or *che-u-ry, che-u-ry, che-u-ry*, introduced or followed by two or three clear, melodious whistles. Two very remarkable things about this song are its *arpeggio* quality, as if it were accompanied by some rare musical instrument, and its ventriloquistic effect. You will sometimes discover a veery, which you have been listening to for some time and have supposed to be at a considerable distance, perched on a tree over your very head. The veery is the smallest of the thrushes, with heavily mottled breast and tawny back, whence it is sometimes called the tawny thrush. Of the song of the veery Burroughs writes: "The soft, mellow flute of the veery fills a place in the chorus of the woods that the song of the vesper-sparrow fills in the chorus of the fields. It is one of the simplest strains to be heard, delighting from the pure element of harmony and beauty it contains."

The handsome oriole (*icterus Baltimore*), to most of us the most conspicuous arrival of May, has already begun to sing from our elm-trees, and will soon commence building his pendent nest. In the South it is said that these birds invariably build on the north and west side of the tree, while in our colder climate it is well known that they generally suspend their nests from boughs looking to the south or east. I would suggest to any of my readers who may care to make the experiment that bright-colored yarn left in an exposed place in the yard would probably result in a brilliant and variegated hang-bird's nest in the elm-tree before the house. Besides the rich, liquid whistles common to both sexes, and heard at all hours of the day, the male oriole possesses a beautiful, protracted warble, which he pours forth generally in the early morning. One of the most remarkable things about the bird is its disappearance about the last of July and its subsequent return towards the last of August, just previous to its departure for the South, when its whistles are again heard for a few days.

Almost the first song to be heard in the woods, at all hours of the day, is the highly accentuated *crescendo* of the oven-bird (*seiurus aurocapillus*). The oven-bird, formerly called the golden-crowned thrush, but now relegated to the family of warblers, is one of the commonest of our woodland birds. It derives its name from its oven-shaped, over-arched nest, which is generally so successfully concealed on the ground that it is considered a great prize by the juvenile collector of birds' eggs. Within a few years it has been discovered that this bird, during the mating season, sometimes indulges in a rare bit of melody, which combines the vivacity of the goldfinch with the rich warble of the purple-finch. This is the first season I have been fortunate enough to hear this love-song of the oven-bird, and, though I had been listening for it and knew what to expect, it was hard to convince myself that so delicious a warble could proceed from an American warbler. The oven-bird, like the crow and the meadow-lark, is a walker, differing in this respect from the great majority of birds, which are hoppers. Its delicate, flesh-colored legs mark it at once as a ground warbler, since the legs of the tree-warbler are black and much stouter and coarser.

As the song of the oven-bird in the woods, so is the song of the yellow-warbler (*dendroica æstiva*) in the orchards and gardens, everywhere to be heard. In Elm Park the other day, I could easily have counted twenty-five or thirty individuals. This bird is very conspicuous, being of a bright, greenish yellow, slightly streaked with black. His song, which for several weeks will be heard constantly, consists of five or six pipes, ending abruptly in a sharp quaver, the whole uttered with great rapidity, but much less musical than a sparrow-song.

A song much resembling that of the yellow-warbler, though considerably shorter and weaker, is that of the beautiful little redstart (*setophaga ruticilla*), another member of the elegant warbler family, which is very abundant in all our woods. The redstart is black above and white beneath, with beautiful patches of bright red on its sides and breast. This bird was formerly classed by ornithologists with the fly-catchers, by reason of its habit of capturing its insect food on the wing, but now it takes its place with the family to which its elegance and brilliant plumage entitle it.

The warbling vireo (*vireo gilvus*), the first of his family to arrive from the South, is a singer of good parts, and of all the birds known to me may most emphatically be said to warble. His song much resembles that of the purple-finch, but contains none of the trills of the latter, and is not nearly so full and round. Somebody has tried to turn it into English by the words *brigadier, brigadier, bridget*, which, perhaps, express very well the accentuation, the number of syllables, and the pauses. Perhaps the most interesting thing about this bird is that it is much more abundant in the city than in more retired localities, seeming to prefer the elms and maples that line our city streets. How few passers-by feel grateful to this little vireo for the delicious music which he lavishes on them from above. In Elm Park the song of these birds can scarcely be missed. The vireos (Latin *viridis*), or greenlets, all have greenish-brown backs, with white beneath, and are a family confined exclusively to the New World. They seem to occupy in ornithology a middle ground between the finches and the warblers.

The fly-catchers, of which the only representative so far mentioned in my letters is the phœbe-bird, belong to the great division of *clamatores*, or screamers, and really have no right to sing at all. The least fly-catcher, or chebec (*empidonax minimus*), may be said strictly to follow the letter of instructions laid down for him by the ornithologists. His sharp, emphatic *chebec* is far from melodious, resembling somewhat one of the commonest utterances of the unmusical English sparrow.

The last bird I shall mention in this letter is the wood-pewee (*contopus virens*), another member of the fly-catcher family, whose long-drawn-out *pe-ee-wee* in sweetness and pathos scarcely yields the palm to many of the *oscines* or singing-birds proper. The wood-pewee, like the field-sparrow, the chewink, and the wood-thrush, sings far into the summer. Its nest, which rivals the humming-bird's in elegance, is made of bark and lichens, and saddled on to the top of a horizontal bough, so that it is almost impossible to distinguish it from an excresence of the tree itself.

I think, in closing, that I cannot do better than quote the last stanza of a poem by Trowbridge on this bird, especially as it contains the most beautiful allusion to the song of the wood-thrush I have ever seen: —

> For so I found my forest bird, —
> The pewee of the loneliest woods, —
> Sole singer in these solitudes,
> Which never robin's whistle stirred,
> Where never blue-bird's plume intrudes.
> Quick darting through the dewy morn,
> The redstart trilled his twittering horn
> And vanished in thick boughs; at even
> Like liquid pearls fresh showered from heaven,
> The high notes of the lone wood-thrush
> Fell on the forest's holy hush;
> But thou all day complainest here, —
>   'Pewee! pewee! peer!'

V.

MAY BIRDS (Continued).

Worcester, May 18, 1887.

My dear Mr. Editor,—While walking yesterday in Hope Cemetery, I heard issuing from the birch woods to the eastward a rich, rolling warble, reminding me somewhat of the song of the robin. I was at once persuaded that these notes could belong only to one bird, the rose-breasted grosbeak (*goniaphea ludoviciana*), one of the rarest and most beautiful of our birds. Following up the song I was soon able to identify the bird with certainty, as he was far from shy, and retained his perch until I was almost under the tree from which he was singing. Whoever has been fortunate enough once to catch a glimpse of the rose-breasted grosbeak is not likely soon to forget him. He is about the size of the robin, black above and light beneath, with a heavy, rather homely beak, whence his name. But this rather unattractive feature is amply counterbalanced by a beautiful rose-blush circular spot in the very centre of his breast, which is very conspicuous and unmistakable against the white.

A friend of mine, I remember, once came across one of these handsome birds, which he had never seen before, in the backwoods of Maine, and using this beautiful mark as a target, sent a rifle-bullet through its heart. The bird's chief ornament was thus the occasion of its death. The female wants the rose-blush mark on the breast, and is altogether a plain, inconspicuous bird, with a brown back and light breast. Some ornithologists profess to see in the subdued tints of the females of nearly all our birds a wise provision of nature, which has clad in plainer and less noticeable attire the sex which is most concerned in the propagation of its kind. They find a similarly wise provision in the law of nature which has conferred such rich musical gifts on the male birds, which are almost entirely denied to the females. The rose-breasted grosbeak is closely allied to the beautiful cardinal grosbeak, — a more southern species, with which most of my readers are probably familiar as a cage-bird, — as well as to the blue-grosbeak of Louisiana. The musical attainments of this bird, as of the cardinal grosbeak, are of a very high order, but his comparative rarity prevents his song being familiar to most of us. I saw only three or four of these birds during the whole of last season, but one individual last June flew into a tree in Elm Park, directly over my head, thus giving me an admirable opportunity to study his song. It reminds one both of the song of the robin and of the rich warble of the oriole, but to my mind is much superior to either.

Another bird, no less striking in appearance than the grosbeak, and much commoner, being in fact rather abundant in all our thick woods, is the brilliant scarlet tanager (*pyranga rubra*). This bird is all the more conspicuous, as his flaming plumage is generally set off in strong relief against the dark pines and hemlocks of the forest, which one almost expects him to ignite as he flashes through them like a living coal. This tanager has jet-black wings, in marked contrast to his brilliant body, but a closely allied species, the summer red-bird (*pyranga æstiva*), which is abundant west of New England, is red all over. The scarlet tanager is common all through the Millstone Hill region, and I often hear there his wild, half-suppressed *chip-cheer*, sounding as if uttered beneath his breath. Besides this note the tanager has also a beautiful warbling song, so much like the robin's that it is often very difficult to distinguish them. There is, however, a certain indescribable wildness about the tanager's voice, harmonizing with the deep, unfrequented woods where he lives, that, after a little study, makes it unmistakable. This bird is a most accomplished ventriloquist, and one of the most experienced and learned students [1] of bird-songs in the State has told me that it is impossible for him to trace home the scarlet tanager by his song alone. The female is of a yellowish-green color, and would never be suspected for a moment of being in any wise related to her brilliant mate.

That the scarlet tanager is not better known than he is, notwithstanding his brilliant plumage, is perhaps not at all surprising, in view of the secluded localities which he generally frequents; but the red-eyed vireo (*vireo olivaceus*) can scarcely be said to leave this excuse open, yet I surmise that not one in ten of my readers ever heard of him. Abundant everywhere in the deep woods, where he is heard in company with the oven-bird, the tanager, and the redstart, and along our city streets, where his song blends with that of the warbling vireo, the purple finch, the yellow warbler, the robin, and the chippee, this little vireo sings constantly his un-

[1] Mr. E. H. Forbush, of Worcester, Mass. — EDS.

assuming, rather monotonous song at all hours of the day, and far into the summer, long after most of the birds have become silent. It is the elegant little nest of this bird which the falling leaves reveal to us in the autumn, suspended from the forked branches of the maple-tree. Samuels finds in the red-eyed vireo a favorite bird. Of him he writes: —

"I feel that no description of mine can begin to do justice to the genial, happy, industrious disposition of this one of our most common, and perhaps best loved birds. From the time of its arrival, about the first week in May, until its departure, about the first week in October, it is seen in the foliage of elms and other shade-trees in the midst of our cities and villages, in the apple-trees near the farm-houses, and in the tall oaks and chestnuts in the deep forests. Everywhere in the New England States, at all hours of the day, from early dawn until evening twilight, his sweet, half-plaintive, half-meditative carol is heard. This consists of the syllables *'wee cheweo turrullet cheweeo*, given in a singularly sweet tone. I know that I am not singular in my preference when I say that, of all my feathered acquaintances, this is the greatest favorite I have. I always loved it, and I can never look upon one after it is killed, no matter how naturally it is preserved, without a sad feeling,—as if it were one of my own most dear friends dead before me."

One of the most delightful arrivals of the last few days, and a favorite bird of mine, is the dainty little Maryland yellow-throat (*geothlypis trichas*). To my mind, he is the prettiest singer of all the warblers, and his lively *pity me, pity me, pity me*, far from expresses the sentiment suggested in the words by which his song is usually translated into English. This bird is olive-green above, with a black head, and white beneath, with a beautiful bright yellow throat, by which he may be easily identified. The yellow-throat is a ground warbler, and is usually found in moist meadows and thickets. This bird is remarkably abundant in Peat Meadow, and from the rifle range this side of the meadow a dozen songs may often be heard at once issuing from as many throats.

The nighthawk (*chordeiles virginianus*), which is really no hawk at all, and the whippoorwill (*antrostomus vocifcrus*) are two closely allied species of birds belonging to the family of goat-suckers (*caprimulgidæ*). Their generic name had its origin in an old superstition in England, founded on the broad, ugly beaks, covered with woolly bristles, which mark the birds of this family. The nighthawk and the whippoorwill look almost exactly alike, both being brown birds, sprinkled with ashy gray, as if they had fallen into an ash-barrel, and it is not surprising that the curiously erroneous idea should prevail in some quarters that the two are simply different sexes of the same bird.

Apart from the fact that they are both nocturnal birds, however, they present the most marked contrasts, both in their general habits and their notes. The whippoorwill is one of the most retired of our birds, inhabiting the densest forests. I often hear him in the woods which line Lake Quinsigamond, and I remember once hearing a regular chorus of their weird utterances at Happy Valley in Boylston. These birds are viewed with much superstitious awe in some parts of the country, and a whippoorwill singing from the ridge-pole of a farm-house is considered a most ominous event. The whippoorwill builds no nest, but deposits its two beautiful cream-colored eggs, which are quite rare and of considerable value, in a depression on the bare ground. The nighthawk is almost a city bird, and its loud, squeaking cry is one of the commonest sounds to be heard everywhere along our city streets in the early evening twilight, as the bird wheels about just above the roofs of the buildings in pursuit of night-flying insects of all kinds. One of the most remarkable things about the nighthawks is the way they have changed their breeding habits, in accordance with the changed conditions of the country, and birds which formerly laid their eggs on rocky ledges in the deep woods are now found depositing them on the flat tin roofs of our Main Street blocks, as a most convenient substitute.

The chimney-swift (*chaetura pelasgia*), generally, but erroneously called the chimney-swallow, is another bird often to be seen in the early evening, circling about far up in the sky. His perfectly blunt tail is sufficient to distinguish him from the family of swallows, to which he is in no wise related. These birds are probably the swiftest of the feathered tribe, and the distance they cover in a single day must be something simply marvellous. It is calculated that during the migrations these birds travel as far as a thousand miles in a single night. The swifts formerly built in hollow trunks of trees, but now build in deserted chimney-flues, from which habit they derive their name. Formerly vast numbers of them built in the chimneys of the old Salisbury mansion on Lincoln Square, and at all hours of the day they could be seen circling about above the chimneys in dense clouds. The chimney-swifts have been with us now for several weeks.

The barn-swallow (*hirundo horreorum*), perhaps the commonest of our swallows, but which generally arrives from the South several weeks later than the white-breasted swallow, may be easily distinguished by his reddish-brown breast and his exceedingly forked tail. This swallow, like the chimney-swift, formerly nested in the hollow trunks of trees.

The eave-swallow, or cliff-swallow (*petrochelidon lunifrons*), is nearly as common as the barn-swallow. In accommodating itself to the advance of civilization, this swallow has very naturally chosen to build its plaster nest outside the barn, under the eaves, as most similar to the ancient cliffs which its ancestors had used for the same purpose.

The smallest of all the swallows and almost the only one whose breeding habits have suffered no change since the white man settled the country, is the little bank-swallow (*cotyle riparia*), which is not very common in this vicinity. This bird, like the kingfisher, still lays its eggs in the middle of the sand-bank, which it reaches by long subterranean passages which it has excavated for itself.

The purple-martin (*progne purpurea*), the largest and handsomest of the swallows, for some inexplicable reason seems to be rather uncommon about Worcester. Whether this is any wise due to the advent of the English sparrow, with which perhaps this bird would be most apt to clash by reason of its similar breeding habits, I am unable to say.

VI.

JUNE BIRDS.

WORCESTER, June 9, 1887.

MY DEAR MR. EDITOR, — Of all months in the year June is the month which all lovers of bird-music can least afford to lose. Before the first of June in this latitude all the birds have come, and very few are silent before the first of July. Since my last letter the most prominent and best known arrivals are the bobolinks, the king-birds, the indigo-birds, the humming-birds, and the cuckoos, the last being always the tardiest of our birds to make their appearance from the South. As the bluebird led the van, so the cuckoo brings up the rear of the great feathered army.

The bobolink (*dolichonyx oryzivorus*), whose rare musical gifts entitle him to be first mentioned in this letter, is one of the most familiar and best loved of our birds. This bird is peculiar to North America and has no even remote kindred in the Old World. He is unique even among our own birds. In the first place he is the only one that has clear white above with black beneath. Then the bobolink's rollicking gush of melody is said to be the only bird-song which the Southern mocking-bird is unable to mimic. A caged mocking-bird will at once become silent when he hears the silvery medley of the bobolink coming up from the meadow before the farm-house. Of this bird's song Samuels writes: "Almost everybody in the North knows the song of the bobolink, and has laughed in spite of himself at the grotesque singer, as, perched on a twig in the cherry-tree by the house, or in the elm by the roadside, or in the alder by the brook, he nodded his head, quivered his wings, opened his mouth, and rattled out the most curious, incomprehensible, jingling, roundabout, careless, joyous, laughable medley that any bird-throat ever uttered."

All my readers are familiar with Bryant's "Robert of Lincoln," in which he trys to turn this song into English poetry. He is hardly so successful, it seems to me, as Wilson Flagg, a practical ornithologist, in his charming little poem entitled "The O'Lincoln Family."

Few birds undergo so complete a change of plumage as the male bobolink at the end of the breeding season. Then he not only loses his voice, but takes on a dull brown dress, in place of his conspicuous black and white attire, and it would be difficult indeed to recognize in him the gayly dressed minstrel of a month before.

Late in August the bobolinks collect in vast flocks, and begin to move southward in their fall migration. During their passage through the Middle States, when they become very fat, they are slaughtered in great quantities for the table, and are there known as reed-birds. In the Southern States they become rice-birds, since they make great havoc in the rice-fields of these States, and again in the Bahamas they play the role of the butter-bird. The bobolinks winter in the West Indies, or even farther south. They summer in Canada, and in New England, and the other Northern States, and every spring throughout this whole region there is scarcely a meadow which is not taken possession of by at least one pair of these birds. The bobolinks are common enough everywhere about Worcester, but I find them especially abundant in the fields and meadows on both sides of Lincoln Street from Adams Square to the Poor Farm.

The king-bird (*tyrannus carolinensis*), largest of the fly-catcher family, is probably as familiar to most of my readers as the bobolink, with his white-tipped tail-feathers, black back, and white breast. He is, perhaps, most noticeable as he sits on the telegraph and telephone wires, darting forth now and then to capture some unwary moth or beetle, and then as quickly regaining his perch. His song is a sharp jingle, not entirely unpleasing to the ear. This bird is, perhaps, best known for his unbounded courage, which leads him to attack even the largest birds of prey, and it is no uncommon sight in the country to see a little king-bird away up in the air in hot pursuit of some hawk or crow. It is said that he sometimes attacks even the eagle, and that the king of birds is obliged to lower his colors to his plucky little assailant.

One of the most interesting recent arrivals, though probably known to but few of my readers, is the beautiful little indigo-bird (*cyanospiza cyanea*). This bird belongs to the great family of finches, and is thus related to the goldfinch and the purple-finch, with which its pretty song and conspicuous plumage would seem to associate it. Its song consists of the syllables *tchee, tchee, tchee,— tchee, tchee, tchee, — tchee, tchee, tchee,* uttered in a peculiar, lisping manner. Unlike most bird-songs, it begins high and loud, and gradually descends, the last notes being scarcely audible. The indigo-bird is generally found in bushy pastures and clearings, and since, like these birds, he sings far into the summer, I am apt to associate him in my mind with the field-sparrow and the chewink. I often hear his song south of Bell Pond and on the south slope of Chandler Hill, and I sometimes hear him in the fields southwest of Adams Square.

The ruby-throated humming-bird (*trochilus colubris*) belongs to the family of *strisores*, or squeakers, like the chimney-swift and the nighthawk. It is well known that the humming-birds are confined exclusively to the New World. The ruby-throated is the only representative of his family found within the boundaries of the United States, while in tropical South America genera, sub-genera, and species are found innumerable, and new ones are being discovered continually. These winged gems are too well known to require more than a passing notice. They come late and leave early, and while they are with us it seems as though their visit to our colder clime could be only accidental, — as if they were continually pining for the more congenial warmth of the tropics whence they come.

The cuckoos (*coccyzi*), like the woodpeckers, belong in ornithology to the order of *scansores*, or climbers, having two pairs of toes opposite each other, instead of three on one side and one on the other. The family is represented in North America by two species, the black-billed and the yellow-billed. The former is rather the more northern of the two, and is, therefore, more abundant about Worcester. They are both large birds, about the size of the brown-thrush, though of rather slenderer and more graceful build, and are light-chestnut above, and white beneath. The American, unlike the European cuckoo, builds a nest of its own, and rears its own offspring. Its nest is a very slight affair, however, and some ornithologists attribute this fact to its near kinship to the European cuckoo. The notes of both our cuckoos are very similar, consisting of the syllables *kow, kow, kow,* or *kru, kru, kru, kru,* reminding one very little of the plain *cuckoo, cuckoo,* of the European bird. Burroughs, when in England, found little satisfaction in the cuckoo's note, which seemed to him a gross plagiarism on the cuckoo-clock. The cuckoo's note has in a remarkable degree the quality of remoteness and introvertedness, and Wordsworth's well-known lines apply equally well to our own bird: —

> While I am lying on the grass
>   Thy twofold shout I hear,
> From hill to hill it seems to pass,
>   At once far off, and near.
>
> The same whom in my school-boy days
>   I listened to; the cry
> Which made me look a thousand ways
>   In bush, and tree, and sky.
>
> To seek thee did I often rove
>   Through woods and on the green;
> And thou wert still a hope, a love;
>   Still longed for, never seen!

To the farmer the call of the cuckoo bodes rain, whence he is in some quarters called the rain-crow.

There are several of our less known warblers which deserve at least a passing notice in these papers. The black and white creeping-warbler (*mniotilta varia*) is rather common in most of our thick woods, where I often hear it in company with the redstart. Its song is very fine and insect-like, more so, perhaps, than that of any other bird, consisting of a lisping rendition of the syllables *wheechee, wheechee, wheechee.*

The black-throated green warbler (*dendroeca virens*) is said generally to be found in pine and hemlock groves, though I am obliged to confess I am as yet unfamiliar with its song. Burroughs and Torrey, however, consider it the best of all the warbler-songs. The latter has turned it into English by the words, *Sleep, sleep, pretty one, sleep.*

Another warbler with whose song I am unfamiliar is the elegant blue yellow-back (*parula americana*), which is said to be common in hardwood groves. I am sure it would amply repay any of my readers to visit the Natural History rooms and inspect the beautifully mounted specimen of this bird, which the society is fortunate enough to possess. The blue yellow-back is the smallest, the daintiest, and most elegant of our warblers.

The black-poll warbler (*dendroeca striata*) is chiefly interesting as being, with the exception of the cuckoo, the last of our birds to usher in the spring. The insect-like *jee, jee, jee* of this warbler is heard everywhere during the last week of May, and the tardiness of his arrival would seem to justify us in supposing that he had come to stay; but he is only a migrant, and in a week or two he has left us as suddenly as he came, and taken wing for the far northern forests, where he breeds. Audubon, who found this bird breeding in the wilds of Labrador, congratulates himself on being the first white man who ever saw its nest and eggs.

I must not omit to mention, also, the beautiful and familiar cedar-bird, or cherry-bird (*ampelis cedrorum*), unmusical though he be. This bird, like that rare winter visitant, the Bohemian chatterer, belongs to the family of waxwings, so called from a horny appendage, like sealing-wax, on the tips of their wings. The cedar-bird is very uncertain in its movements and migrations, which are apparently independent of the weather, and flocks of them are often seen in mid-winter along the city streets, feeding on the buds of the cedar-tree.

The last bird which I shall mention in these papers is the little spotted sandpiper (*tringoides macularius*). He is the only representative of a large family that stays with us to breed, and is found on the shores of every body of water in New England. He makes his appearance as early as the first week in April, or as soon as the ice breaks up in our rivers and ponds, and his peculiar *peet-weet, peet-weet,* which is heard all through the season, is easily recognized.

I cannot forbear in closing to quote the first and last stanzas of a delightful little poem on this bird by Celia Thaxter.

> Across the narrow beach we flit,
>   One little sandpiper and I;
> And fast I gather, bit by bit,
>   The scattered driftwood bleached and dry.
> The wild waves reach their hands for it,
>   The wild wind raves, the tide runs high,
> As up and down the beach we flit, —
>   One little sandpiper and I.
>
> . . . .
>
> Comrade, where wilt thou be to-night
>   When the loosed storm breaks furiously?
> My driftwood fire will burn so bright!
>   To what warm shelter canst thou fly?
> I do not fear for thee, though wroth
>   The tempest rushes through the sky;
> For are we not God's children both,
>   Thou little sandpiper and I?

VII.

MIDSUMMER SONGSTERS.

WORCESTER, July 28th, 1887.

DEAR MR. EDITOR, — With most birds, their singing is confined to the seasons of mating and of nesting. After the young birds have left the nest, the parents generally become silent. Who ever heard the gushing, rollicking song of the bobolink in the month of August, or even after the middle of July? Such an event would be indeed a strange and unaccountable phenomenon, for the bobolinks are always very careful to have their young fully fledged and out of the nest before the mower comes to cut the grass in the meadows and threaten the destruction of their dwellings, together with their precious contents. Some birds, however, rear several broods in the season, and may sometimes be found nesting even as late as the last of July, while all birds whose first efforts at raising their quota of young have for any reason miscarried are pretty sure to make a second attempt, which often carries them far into the summer. Thus the wood-thrush, when the first nest has been robbed, a thing which often happens by reason of its exposed position, will sometimes continue singing almost to the middle of August.

Until recently the robins have been in full song, and within a few days I have heard sing fitfully and as if by accident, the yellow-warbler, the bluebird, the warbling-vireo, the cat-bird, the pigeon-woodpecker, and the golden-robins. The song of the yellow-warbler interested me particularly. I had not heard him for a month and was therefore much surprised yesterday to hear his song issuing from the moist thickets of Peat Meadow. All the notes were there, but the song was delivered in a listless and perfunctory manner, as if the bird had little heart for singing. It seemed to be a reminiscence of the gay springtime, expressing no present joy but rather a regret for the joyful days that were gone. Until within a day or two I have not heard for over a month the rich warble of the golden-robin. It is now their second springtime. It is ·a well-known fact, though very difficult to explain, that these birds after remaining silent for nearly a month, again become vocal in August just before their departure for the South. The loud squeaking and booming of the nighthawk is still one of the commonest evening sounds along our city streets, and the weird cry of the whippoorwill is still common enough along the shores of Lake Quinsigamond, but these goat-suckers are not to be classed with singing-birds at all.

The most persistent and reliable midsummer songsters, however, are the song, vesper, and field sparrows, the chewink, the indigo-bird, the wood-pewee, and the red-eyed vireo. These are the midsummer and late summer minstrels *par excellence*. Their singing seems to be entirely independent of their breeding habits. In the extracts from his journal entitled "Summer," edited by Mr. H. G. O. Blake, Thoreau writes: "Some birds are poets and sing all summer. They are the true singers. Any man can write verses in the love season. We are most interested in those birds that sing for the love of the music and not of their mates; who meditate their strains and amuse themselves with singing; the birds whose strains are of deeper sentiment."

The song-sparrow deserves especial praise for singing so late in the season, and there is probably no other of our birds that from first to last contributes so much to the general chorus. Appearing sometimes as early as the first week in March, he begins singing from the first moment of his arrival, and continues to regale us with his lively and spirited melody, sometimes until the first of September. At both extremities of the season his voice is often the only one to be heard from far or near. He sings, too, all day long, except perhaps at high noon, and as if conscious that such persistent singing, if unvaried, might in time become tiresome to the listener, the song-sparrow gives us some six or seven variations, which sometimes follow one another in rapid succession. One of these variations, consisting of a long and peculiarly liquid whistle, immediately after the introductory note, and before the concluding trills, is especially beautiful. Thoreau, in the book above quoted, writes: " R. W. E. [Ralph Waldo Emerson] imitates the wood-thrush by '*He willy willy — ha willy willy — O willy, O.*' The song-sparrow is said to be imitated in New Bedford thus: '*Maids, maids, maids, hang on your tea-kettle — ettle ettle — ettle — ettle.*' "

The vesper-sparrow, or bay-winged bunting, also comes early, and we should indeed be grateful to him for continuing his sweet, melodious trills through into the heat of the dog-days. I still hear him singing as persistently as ever, whenever my walk takes me to the high, open pastures beyond Sunnyside.

Thoreau writes in his journal, under date of June 23, 1856: "To New Bedford with R——. Baywings sang morning and evening about R——'s house, often resting on a beanpole, and dropping down and running and singing on the bare ground amid the potatoes their note somewhat like *Come here, here — there, there* (then three rapid notes) — *quick, quick, quick, or I'm gone.*"

The long, vibrating whistle of the field-sparrow, or bush-sparrow, as John Burroughs calls him, is one of the characteristic sounds of midsummer on the bushy hillside. Thoreau, writing of summer, says: "Maybe the huckleberry-bird best expresses the season, or the red-eye. What subtile differences between one season and another!" I was long in doubt what bird Thoreau meant by the huckleberry-bird, but in view of this remark, and since he nowhere mentions the field-sparrow by name, there can be little doubt that this bird was meant. The local and popular names of birds, as of flowers, are infinite. This bird may be heard any day along the hillside east of Peat Meadow.

It is no wonder that the little red-eyed vireo keeps on singing his simple, rather monotonous ditty all through the summer, and almost up to the time of his departure for the South, about the second week in September. His song, which he carols all day long, as he flits about among the leaves of the maple in pursuit of his insect food, seems to be treated by him as a part of the business of the day, and is in no wise expressive of undue emotion and exuberance of spirits, as is the case with the singing of most birds.

That curious harlequin, in his pied dress, the chewink or ground-robin, or towhee bunting, is another bird I always hear almost till the close of summer, usually in company with the field-sparrow. Even after he has abandoned his sparrow-like song, he still gives us his hardly less musical call-note *towhee*, until he leaves for the South in October.

The sweet, pathetic *pe-ee-wee* of the wood-pewee is now heard not only in the deep woods, which are the bird's proper habitation, but on the city lawns as well; for at this season the pewees, like many other forest birds, leave their woodland retreats after the young have left the nest, and seek their food in the gardens of our cities, where they find insects in great abundance. Speaking of the peculiar pathos of the pewee's voice, I remember one ornithologist who derides the sentimentality of the poet who conceived this bird to be weighed down with sorrow and woe. Notwithstanding the peculiar structure of its windpipe, the ornithologist assures us that the pewee manages to enjoy life about as well as the majority of birds. All birds, however, considering the manifold perils to which they are exposed, seem to be remarkably cheerful and light-hearted.

It is doubtful if many of our song-birds

die a natural death. What with hawks and snakes and the perils inseparably connected with their migrations, not to speak of the small boy with his murderous gun, they pass indeed a precarious and uncertain existence. Then, as we all know, the domestic cat is responsible for only too large a share of bird fatalities. The eggs and helpless young, moreover, are · peculiarly liable to disaster. The common red squirrel is a miscreant who is especially fond of birds' eggs, and the crow, blue-jay, and many other species of birds are addicted to the disreputable habit of preying on the eggs of their smaller neighbors. We must remember, however, that it is thus that nature prevents the undue increase of all species of animals, and thus works out her own Malthusian theory. It is only when the balance is disturbed by the introduction of new and adventitious causes of destruction that we need fear the extermination of any species of animals. Must not the fatalities among our birds caused by the small boy and the purveyor of birds' feathers for hat decorations be classed in this category?

To revert, however, from this digression to summer bird-songs, the most characteristic and typical summer songster is the indigo-bird. This beautiful little bird, whose deep blue plumage is much darker than that of the bluebird, comes so late in the season that it is only right that he should continue to sing for us through the summer.

He sings all through the livelong summer day, and his song, consisting of a lisping rendition of the syllable *tehee*, *tehee*, *tehee-tehee*, *tehee*, *tehee-tehee*, *tehee*, *tehee*, is as much of a midsummer sound as the chirping of a cricket. I heard him yesterday singing loud and clear at the end of the woods, just north of Sunnyside, his being the only bird-song within hearing. I am also pretty sure to hear him in the fields west of Adams Square. I will quote in conclusion the following extract from Thoreau's journal: "June 9, 1857, P. M. To Violet, Sorrel, and Calla

Swamp. In the sprout land, beyond the red huckleberry, an indigo-bird, which chirps about me as if it had a nest there. This is a splendid and marked bird, high colored as is the tanager, looking strange in this latitude. Glowing indigo. Wilson says it sings, not like most other birds, in the morning and evening chiefly, but also in the middle of the day. In this I notice it is like the tanager, the other fiery-plumaged bird. They seem to love the heat. It probably had its nest in one of these bushes."

VIII.

BIRD NOMENCLATURE. — SOME ENGLISH AND AMERICAN BIRDS.

WORCESTER, Aug. 8, 1887.

MY DEAR MR. EDITOR, — When our forefathers settled this country they named most of the birds they found here after those that had been familiar to them in Old England. Thus the common migratory thrush (*turdus migratorius*) they named the robin, because that bird's reddish-brown breast and familiar, sociable ways reminded them of the English robin redbreast, that much loved bird which the pathetic old ballad of "The Babes in the Woods" had immortalized. The famous European skylark, which has inspired so many poets in the old world, lent its name to the bird which the early colonists found inhabiting the meadows along the streams of the New World. Our crow-blackbird, redwinged blackbird, and cow-blackbird, derived their names from the English thrush which bears that name. In like manner our American chimney-swift was named from the English chimney-swallow, and our purple-martin from the English window-martin, or cliff-swallow. Our summer yellowbird or thistle-bird, was called the goldfinch, and our purple-finch the linnet. Our ruffed grouse was called the partridge, and our American partridge the quail. So after the English redstart, a bird nearly allied to the robin redbreast, one of our wood-warblers, a family peculiar to the New World, was named. The cuckoos, wrens, and nuthatches are other familiar instances.

From an ornithological point of view, however, these popular names were sometimes glaring misnomers, and, indeed, were often based upon very superficial resemblances. Thus our American robin's nearest congener in Europe is the blackbird. Both are thrushes; they are of about the same size, and, according to the Duke of Argyle, their songs bear a very strong resemblance to each other. The English robin is about half the size of ours, and is no thrush at all, but belongs, like the nightingale, to the family of European warblers. I have observed that domestics newly arrived from the Old World always call our robins thrushes, as indeed they should. The nearest relative of the English robin in this country is the bluebird. They both have reddish-brown breasts, are of about the same size, and in general resemble one another very closely. Yet I was much surprised to see in an English encyclopædia that the American bluebird was known as the English robin. The error of the learned author of the article was in a measure excused by the error of our ancestors.

In ornithology our meadow-lark is not a lark, but an American starling. Though he is a large, handsome bird, with a conspicuous yellow breast, his song consists merely of a long, wavering whistle, which is always uttered from the ground, and which bears not the slightest resemblance to the copious notes of the skylark, which he showers down upon us from far up in the sky. The only true lark to be found in these parts is the shore-lark, which with us is only a winter bird of passage, and which, even in its summer haunts in the far North, is said to be possessed of rather inferior musical gifts. Recently, however, in the vicinity of the Yellowstone Park, a new lark, called Sprague's lark, has been discovered, whose song is said to be unequalled by his celebrated European cousin. I saw the other day, in a New York newspaper, that the skylark has recently been introduced into some parts of New York State with complete success. What a substitute this bird would have been for the English sparrow!

Our beautiful purple-martin has no near congener in the European avifauna, our common cliff or eave swallow corresponding to the English window-martin. They both build their hemispherical plaster nests on the sides of steep cliffs, or under the eaves of houses and barns. Shakspeare's well-known lines in Macbeth apply equally well to our own bird: —

> This guest of summer,
> The temple-haunting martlet, does approve,
> By his loved mansionry, that the heaven's breath
> Smells wooingly here. No jutty, frieze,
> Buttress, nor coigne of vantage, but this bird
> Hath made his pendent bed, and procreant cradle;
> Where they most breed and haunt, I have observed,
> The air is delicate.

It is an interesting and curious fact that while in this country the swift builds in chimneys, in England he builds in barns, while the English swallow, corresponding to our barn-swallow, builds in chimneys. This accounts for our swift being commonly called the chimney-swallow.

Many of our birds, however, especially those which had no European representative, were named from the real or fancied resemblance of their songs or call-notes to certain articulate words or sounds. On this principle of onomatopœia the chewink, the wood-pewee, the phœbe bird, the chicadee, the bobolink, and the veery received their names. The last-mentioned bird was undoubtedly a veery long before he was a Wilson's thrush. Perhaps the most remarkable of our birds in this respect, however, is the whippoorwill, whose weird nocturnal cry is as easily turned into English as the chirping of the katydid. The Indians, however, translated it into "wish-ton-wish," which, perhaps, would be the better version; and Cooper, in his novel by that name, tells us that this bird is in some quarters vulgarly called "the whippoorwill."

It has probably been observed by most of my readers that the nearer you are to the bird, the more difficult it is to distinguish the words of the English translation.

On the comparative merits of the English and American song-birds, John Burroughs, in his "Fresh Fields," writes: —

"I could well understand, after being in England a few days, why, to English travellers, our songsters seem inferior to their own. They are much less loud and vociferous; less abundant and familiar; one needs to woo them more; they are less recently out of the wilderness; their songs have the delicacy and wildness of most woodsy farms, and are as plaintive as the whistle of the wind. They are not so happy a race as the English songsters, as if life had more trials for them, as doubtless it has, in their enforced migrations and in the severer climate with which they have to contend. On the whole, I may add that I did not anywhere in England hear so fine a burst of bird-song as I have heard at home, and I listened long for it and attentively. Not so fine in quality, though perhaps greater in quantity."

Among English travellers Burroughs refers particularly to the Duke of Argyle, who contributed to Frazer's Magazine for 1880 two very interesting papers entitled "Some First Impressions of America."

These papers dealt chiefly with nature

in this country, and the Duke, who is a most accomplished ornithologist, did not forget the birds. He writes that, though he was in the woods and fields of Canada and the States in the richest moment of spring, he heard little of that burst of song with which he had been familiar in England. I was surprised, however, in reading these articles to find that some of our finest singers he does not seem to have heard at all. He makes no mention whatever of the wood-thrush, or the veery, or the bobolink, or the rose-breasted grosbeak, or of many others of our best singers. He does admit that the American robin, though, as he maintains, inferior to the English blackbird, is much more familiar, and therefore much oftener heard. His letters, on the whole, are delightful, and I am sure will amply repay any one who takes the trouble to read them. The humming-bird, which he had searched for long in vain, he at last discovers during a trip to Niagara Falls, and his delight is infinite. He thinks the bird sets off the falls perfectly. How apt is the description of the humming-bird, "a vibratory haze"! The sight of a goldfinch fills him with enthusiasm, and he exclaims, "An American goldfinch, indeed!"

According to Gilbert White's charming book, "On the Natural History of Selborne," which is as much of an English classic as Izaak Walton's "Complete Angler," the linnets and sparrows of England are rather weak singers. How different here! The purple-finch, goldfinch, indigo-bird, rose-breasted grosbeak, the peabody bird, the song, vesper, and field sparrows, all of them superior songsters, are included in this family. As for the thrushes, there are in England only three species, the missal-thrush, or throstle, the song-thrush, or mavis, and the blackbird. Our robin's song, according to Burroughs, is scarcely inferior to any of them, while they have in England no birds whatever answering to our mocking-bird, brown-thrush, catbird, wood-thrush, and veery.

Our vireos are a family peculiar to the

New World, and have no representatives whatever in Europe. Neither have the orioles or the tanagers, or the bobolinks, all of them among the most musical of our birds.

On the other hand, the European warblers, to which family the nightingale belongs, are not represented at all in the New World. The American warblers, which, properly speaking, are not warblers at all, are weak singers, and have nothing in common with the celebrated Old World warblers. According to Burroughs, however, in England at least, the nightingale is very rare; and in his chapter in "Fresh Fields" entitled "A Search for a Nightingale" he gives us an amusing account of his desperate though fruitless endeavor to find that bird.

The skylark, too, at least in the settled parts of this country, has no proper representative, so that the two most famous Old World songsters are denied to the New World. Thus has nature to the Eastern and Western Continent dealt out her gifts with an even and impartial hand.

IX.

THE BIRDS OF PRINCETON.

PRINCETON, June 20, 1889.

MY DEAR MR. EDITOR, — Having passed the last few days in the Worcester County hill town of Princeton, I have been tempted to send you this letter on the birds I have heard sing here at this season of the year, when nearly all our wild birds sing at their best. I am particularly prompted to do this, as it will give me an opportunity to inform local ornithologists that the hermit-thrush, a bird well known for the beauty of its song throughout the White Mountains and the more northern districts of Maine, is to be found breeding and singing on our own Wachusett.

In the first place, as was to be expected, I have heard sing in Princeton nearly all the birds we hear sing in Worcester. The scarlet tanager, the indigo-bird, the king-bird, the wood-thrush, and the humming-bird, which had long escaped me, I have at last succeeded in finding. But there are others which still remain unfound. The chief of these are the veery, or Wilson's thrush, the warbling-vireo, the rose-breasted grosbeak, the red-shouldered blackbird, the crow blackbird, the barn-swallow, the white-breasted swallow, and the night-hawk. On the other hand, there are many species of birds, the individuals of which are much more numerous here than at home.

Of all Princeton birds, the most abundant, persistent, and self-asserting is the chewink. Chewinkville, or Towheetown, would be a most appropriate denomination of Princeton upon any ornithological system of nomenclature of our Worcester County towns. Then the sweet-singing vesper-sparrow is to be found everywhere, pouring forth most lavishly his beautiful lisping ditty, as might naturally be expected in a high, breezy country like that of Princeton. While in Worcester we hear him only on the more distant hills about the city, here he is heard on the town common itself, where he actually takes the place of the obnoxious English sparrow,— a bird which, I omitted to mention, is not included in the avifauna of this town. In Worcester the purple-finch and bluebird are occasionally heard, but here we hear these delicious songsters along the village street on every side. I use the word " delicious " in speaking of the song of the bluebird advisedly, for though I had never known it before, I have now discovered that he is a singer of no mean ability. His singing is almost as profuse as the robin's, and he will sometimes continue singing from the same perch half an hour at a time in the most impassioned manner. Though I miss here the pretty warble of the warbling-vireo, his place is easily supplied by the purple-finch, whose song, though similar, is somewhat superior to his. I never in my life heard such singing from that much under-estimated thrush, the American robin, as here in Princeton. The Princeton air would seem to have purified and exalted his voice, and his kinship to the veery and hermit-thrush is made manifest.

In Worcester the pretty goldfinch, the little yellow bird with the black wings, is not very abundant. Here he is seen flying in all directions with his pretty dipping flight, and uttering his canary-like twitter. The handsome meadow-lark is not uncommon, though found in nothing like such abundance as along the intervals of the Blackstone River in the towns below Worcester. But the merry bobolink pours down his rollicking song from over our heads in every meadow. Here you do not go out of town to seek him, and the best place I know to hear him is from the east piazza of the Wachusett House and from Mr. Bullock's pretty cottage. In July and August, when the town will be visited by crowds of people from the city, the bobolink will have become tuneless, but we hope that his music is appreciated by the few fortunate enough to be already here. Another bird, however, of a very different temper from the bobolink's, the whippoorwill, or the wish-ton-wish, as he was called by the Indians, is heard every evening from the village common, and he will continue to emit throughout the summer his weird, sepulchral cry for the benefit of the visitors of July and August.

About Princeton his near congener, the nighthawk, does not contest the field with him, but leaves the whippoorwill to his solitary glory.

One of the handsomest and most musical of our wood-warblers, the tiny Maryland yellow-throat, which I had hardly expected to find here in Princeton, as he is generally found in low, swampy places, is not uncommon, and his lively *twittitee, twittitee, twittitee*, often greets my ear. The black-and-white creeping-warbler is also often seen here, as is the redstart, whose brisk trill so often salutes you on going out of the open into the forest. The chimney-swifts are very abundant, the chimneys of nearly every farm-house seeming to be repositories of their nests. Of the swallows, the cliff or eave swallow seems to be the prevailing species; the bank-swallows, I am told, are not uncommon, but the white-breasted and the barn are very rare.

Yesterday, while sitting in the stony pasture back of the Mt. Pleasant House, where the well-known authoress " H. H." is said to have passed much of her time during her yearly visits to Princeton, we could not help remarking the peculiar sense of wildness and remoteness which the ringing, vibrating song of the bush-sparrow produced on the mind. This little bird, about the size of the chipping-sparrow, is the least known of all our common sparrows, but it is hard to understand how his clear, ringing whistle can fail to attract attention.

Wilson Flagg, the pioneer of popular ornithologists, writing some thirty years ago, tells us that the voice of the quail or bob-white is no longer heard in the land, — that, being a permanent resident with us, he is destroyed in vast numbers by the severity of our winters, and now that the taste of the epicure and the gun of the fowler are thrown into the scale against him, the quail's speedy extermination is at hand. My Worcester experience would most certainly point to the verification of Flagg's predictions, but here in Princeton it is very different. "*Bob-white,*" or "*More wet,*" as it is sometimes translated, cheery and strong, greets you from every pasture, meadow, and hillside. It may be that the past open winter explains this unusual abundance of the toothsome quail, — whereof all sportsmen and epicures take notice!

The crow is more abundant here than in Worcester, and seems even more wild, savage, and unapproachable. According to Thoreau, these birds embody the departed spirits of the old Indian sagamores. This is certainly a more poetical explanation of their hostility to the white man than to attribute it to the effect of the white man's gun.

As for the thrushes, the robins, the brown-thrushes, and the cat-birds are as abundant about Princeton as they are in the neighborhood of Worcester. As for the smaller thrushes, the sylvan minstrels *par excellence*, the wood-thrush is heard constantly in the grove just northwest of the village. The veery, which I have heard repeatedly this season and last in the peat-meadow woods near Worcester, and which is, on the whole, a common bird in that vicinity, I have failed to hear at all in Princeton. This was hardly unexpected to me, as I knew that the veery generally lives in low woods near ponds, and there are no ponds near Princeton except Wachusett Pond, the other side of the mountain, which I have not yet visited. Now the hermit-thrush is closely allied both to the wood-thrush and the veery, but belongs to the Canadian fauna, while the other two belong to the Apalachian. It is a well-known fact, however, that on the sides of mountains we often find birds and flowers alike which properly belong to regions much further north, the difference in altitude corresponding to the difference in latitude, so that the climates of the northern low lands and of the southern high lands are the same. Moreover I had seen the common slate-colored snow-bird, which is especially characteristic of the Canadian fauna, near the summit of Wachusett in August, and felt convinced that it must have nested there, as it was too early for the fall migrations. Now, if the snow-bird nested there, it was fair to suppose that the hermit-thrush nested there also, and might therefore be heard singing up on the mountain in the month of June. Accordingly I took a trip to the mountain yesterday with the express purpose of solving this interesting problem, if possible. But I had never heard the song of the hermit and had never been able to obtain a satisfactory description of it either from the books or from persons who had heard it. Some authorities compare the hermit's song to that of the veery, others to that of the wood-thrush. I considered, however, that I knew thoroughly, and in all their variations, the songs of these two birds, and I felt sure that I should recognize at once as belonging to this wonderful family, embracing the veery, the wood-thrush, the hermit-thrush, the olive-back thrush, and the gray-cheeked thrush, any song that did actually belong to it. The olive-backed and gray-cheeked are arctic thrushes, so that if I heard the songs of any thrush belonging to this family which I had never heard before, it would be the song of the hermit.

I reached the summit about six o'clock in the evening. On the way up I heard oven-birds and wood-pewees at frequent intervals. I was also much delighted at finding again, near the top, my snow-birds of last summer. This time I was sure they were nesting there, as was plainly shown by their demonstrations while I remained in their neighborhood. On the way up, too, I was encouraged by hearing a whistle which seemed to answer Burroughs's description of the whistle of the hermit. Of course the return down the mountain would furnish the true test, as it would then be just the time of day when all the thrushes of this family are most likely to sing. Accordingly, about half-past six, I slowly began my descent down the bridle-path. The oven-birds seemed never to tire of singing, though I was, in my impatience, almost tired of hearing them.

I had now gone nearly half-way down, and was getting pretty thoroughly discouraged, for I had little hope of hearing them in the lower zone of the mountain. Suddenly, away off to the eastward, but brought to my ears with perfect clearness by the strong east wind, a song arose once, twice, and yet again, until I finally had heard at least eight or ten strains. Then the angry cry of a blue-jay was heard in the same direction, and the singing ceased. I waited half an hour to hear it again, but in vain. I shall return to the mountain tomorrow evening, and hope to hear it a second time; but it would not be necessary in order to convince me more positively that I had heard the hermit-thrush. There is no possibility of confounding it with the veery; the three or four simple bars of the veery's beautiful song have nothing in common with it. It is more like the song of the wood-thrush, but with all the disagreeable features eliminated. It is a continuous, not an interrupted song like that of the wood-thrush. Then the hermit's song is much simpler than his, and wants the jingles and staccato notes of the wood-thrush's song, which are generally considered such blemishes. Then there is absolutely nothing corresponding to the beautiful *airoee* of the wood-thrush. The song I heard consisted of three soft melodious whistles in the same key, followed immediately by three more notes in a very different key. The whole was repeated in rapid succession until it ceased altogether. That it was the hermit-thrush I am sure, and this bird must now be added to the list of birds who nest and rear their young in Worcester county. But I must hear the song again before I am willing to yield it precedence over our own incomparable veery.

X.

OFF CAPE COD.

WHALING IN MASSACHUSETTS BAY.

PROVINCETOWN, BARNSTABLE COUNTY,
Aug. 12, 1887.

MY DEAR MR. EDITOR, — Since my arrival in this old fishing-town, whales have been the absorbing topic of conversation, not only among the transient summer-boarders, but among the permanent residents as well. A few days before I came, a large school of fin-back whales, for the first time in two years, made its appearance at the entrance of Massachusetts Bay, and ever since there has been great excitement here. Several of the guests of the Gifford House, the hotel where I am stopping, had been out whaling, and reported rare sport. The unvarying verdict has been that there was nothing to be compared with it for a moment. So your correspondent, thinking that such an opportunity ought not to be missed, turned out at 4.30 yesterday morning, and walking down to Union wharf, found there the stanch little steamer, "A. B. Nickerson," J. S. Nickerson commander, all ready to set out for the day's whaling. The morning was somewhat cloudy, but the wind was southwest, and everything promised a pleasant day. Besides the captain and crew, there were on board a Marlboro editor and his son, a Boston provision merchant, and myself. The Boston man had been out the day before and had been so infatuated with the sport that he could not forego its repetition. The editor, perched upon the hurricane-deck, spent most of the time taking voluminous notes, and I trust his Marlboro paper may escape the notice of your readers, so that all indivious comparisons of our respective efforts may be avoided.

Steaming out of the magnificent harbor of Provincetown, the only harbor on a lee shore within two hundred miles, we are soon off the Race Point lighthouse, which guards the tip end of Cape Cod. As we stand out to sea, the low, sandy coast-line of the back of the cape comes into full view. Away off to the southeast we can just make out the celebrated Highland lighthouse, one of the three " primary lights " of New England. This is the first light that greets the trans-atlantic voyager on entering Massachusetts Bay. Five miles nearer and easily distinguishable, we see the terrible Peaked (pronounced Picket) Hills bar, with its important life-saving station. This is the most dangerous point on the whole coast, and never a winter passes without leaving many a wreck on these insidious sand-bars, which extend nearly a mile out to sea. During the Revolutionary War H. M. S. " Somerset," one of the British men-of-war that had covered the red-coats while crossing to Bunker Hill, and afterwards set fire to Charlestown, was wrecked at the Peaked Hills, to the great joy of the people of the Cape, to whom this vessel had long been a terror. There were more than four hundred souls on board, many of whom were swallowed up by the sea, and their bodies buried in Deadmen's Hollow, near by. The survivors, among them Captain Aubrey, the commander of the vessel, were marched to Boston as prisoners-of-war by the Barnstable militia. The vessel was thrown up high on the beach, and after a few years was wholly buried in the sand. Within two or three years the constantly shifting sands, after more than a hundred years, again revealed to view the live-oak timbers of the old war-ship. Many are the relics in Provincetown obtained by the townspeople during the temporary exhumation. At the present time the vessel is again imbedded in sand to the depth of nearly thirty feet. This is only one of the innumerable shipwrecks to be charged to the account of this bar.

An old sea-captain told me how, not many years ago, he saw an Italian brig, the "Giovanne," dashed to pieces at the Peaked Hills, and all but one of her crew drowned before his eyes. No living soul could help them, as no life-boat could possibly get through the great foaming breakers which rolled in more than thirty feet high. He said the captain, a great, powerful fellow, several times swam almost up to the shore, but was as often swept back by the undertow. At last he was seen to give up the unequal contest, throw up his hands, and sink below the waves; and after the storm his body was thrown up on the beach, together with those of his crew.

Within a few years, in the month of November, three of the crew of the lifeboat, including the captain, all Provincetown men, were drowned while trying to reach a stranded vessel, a part of whose crew they had already saved. This was the first wreck on the coast after the acquittal of the captain on the charge of cowardice. He had been thus accused because he had refused to put out to a shipwrecked vessel, while a volunteer crew from Provincetown manned the life-boat and rescued the imperilled crew. On his acquittal, however, he took the first opportunity offered to redeem himself, and expiated by his life any past offence of which he might have been guilty.

Before the establishment of the life-saving station, moreover, many a poor fellow whom the waves had spared died of cold and exposure while wandering about in midwinter over the barren wastes of sand which stretch back for over two miles towards Provincetown. But enough of these sad stories of shipwreck and death, which are only too common on this coast.

Before we were five miles beyond Race Point we heard from the man on the lookout above the inspiring cry of "There she blows!" and before long, whales could be seen spouting in all directions, rolling and tossing like great porpoises. It is a great mistake to suppose that whales spout out great volumes of water, as I remember they were represented as doing in the pictures in the geographies. They really spout out no water at all, but the slight spray which is usually seen is the water above their blow-holes, which is forced into the air when the whale exhales.

It may be well right here to describe the peculiar method of killing the fin-back whale, the only whale common on our coast. The harpoon and lance, which are so effective against the sperm, right, and humpback whales, are of very little avail against the fin-back. This whale is long and slender, and "just made for running," as an old whaler told me. When harpooned they will "run the nails out of a boat in no time," going at the rate of almost a mile a minute. A few years ago some young men from the town, who had been foolish enough to harpoon a fin-back, narrowly escaped drowning, being picked up by a passing vessel just as their boat was sinking. Therefore in killing this whale a bomb-lance, a comparatively recent invention, is now always employed. This lance is hollow and charged with powder. It is fired out of a heavy gun or blunderbuss, the powder in the gun igniting a fuse at the end of the lance, which explodes in about fourteen seconds. If the lance has been fired into a vital part, the explosion generally results in the speedy death of the whale.

Although the whales were so numerous, we at first had considerable trouble in getting a shot at them. These fin-back whales are in the habit of spouting five or six times, and then, having filled their lungs with air, they go down to the bottom to feed, often remaining there for a long time. Unless, therefore, you are pretty near them when they first come up, it is impossible to get near enough to shoot them. At last, as luck would have it, a whale comes up to spout for the first time within an eighth of a mile of us. All steam is crowded on, and off we dash in the direction of the whale. Again he rises to blow, and again and again. We are now very near him, and the fifth time he seems to the novice to present a capital shot, being less than a rod distant. The noise of his blowing is like a locomotive letting off steam, and we can trace the outline of his vast body long after he has disappeared beneath the surface. On board there is the intensest excitement. The captain and mate, standing far out on the bowsprit-like bridge, with guns in hand, share the excitement. Will the whale blow again? That is the all-important question which agitates us. If he does it will be our last chance, as it will be his sixth blowing. But the suspense is of short duration. Just ahead of us his head comes slowly into view. At full speed we dash up alongside, and before his ponderous body is again submerged two bomb-lances enter it just behind the left shoulder. We are at once all on the alert, listening for the explosion of the lance. We hear nothing but the dashing of the waves against the steamer's sides, and it is evident that the lance has failed to explode. Still the whale must be seriously injured. We strain our eyes in every direction for the next blowing, for a wounded whale is generally obliged to come up very often to breathe. Soon we see a whale blow an eighth of a mile off our starboard bow, and the man at the look-out declares it to be the wounded whale. He knows it, he says, because there is "something queer about his spout." So after him we tear, and for at least an hour continue to pursue him. At last the captain, in great disgust, and with difficulty repressing his angry feelings towards the man at the masthead, declares we are after the wrong whale, and might as well return home as follow him out to sea any further. So we turn around, considerably crestfallen, having given up all hope of ever seeing the wounded whale again. In the meantime I retired to the cabin for a nap, having made up my mind that whaling was over for the day. Before long, however, I am aroused by a great commotion on deck, and rushing up the companion-way find that a whale whose spout was flecked with blood has just been seen not more than a quarter of a mile away on our port bow. From this time to the death of the whale I never saw such excited men as those on board the steamer, with the possible exception of the mate, an old whaler, who seemed to be reasonably cool. As for the captain, he appeared to be the most excited man on board. Well, we soon succeeded in getting another shot, and this time, as before, the lance failed to explode, and off goes the whale with undiminished speed. The next time he rises, however, his spout is more deeply tinged with blood than before. Again we steam after him at full speed, and soon come up alongside as he rises to blow. This time, thinking the end is near, and fearing that the whale will sink when dead, the captain casts a harpoon into him. Off he rushes with eight hundred feet of rope behind, with the buoy attached to the rope dancing along through the water at a very lively rate. It soon becomes plain that the whale is not going to die so easily. We attempt to get another shot, but find it even more difficult than before. It is impossible to tell what direction the whale is going to take. Now he appears on our port and now on our starboard bow, and we are unable to get anywhere near him. Finally the captain, fuming and swearing, and declaring that even now we shall lose the whale, rope and all, calls down the man at the masthead, whom he takes severely to task for his inability to follow the whale under water, mounts aloft himself, and in stentorian tones shouts out his orders to the man at the wheel. Double caution is now necessary to prevent the rope getting foul of our rudder, which untoward accident would very speedily put an end to the chase. Every time the whale rises to spout the waves are crimson with his blood for many feet around, and the blood is plainly seen pouring out of the holes in his sides, made by the lances. Once he comes up to spout directly under the vessel, and the shock of the collision nearly throws us off our feet. The front deck is covered with blood from his spout. Finally the mate, who all this time has remained stationed on the bridge in front, succeeds in getting another shot, and a dull report tells us that the lance has exploded. According to all precedents the whale should have died at once then and there. The mate can scarcely believe his eyes when, a couple of minutes later, a bloody spout on our port bow announces that the whale has still considerable life left. It is nearly half an hour before another shot is secured. Again the lance explodes, and again the whale disappears from view. The mate, in great wrath, with a mighty oath, shouts out to the captain aloft that he has fired his last shot, and, if he has not killed the whale this time, the captain has got to come down and kill him himself. For more than a minute nothing is seen; then the whale's back appears above the surface of the water, a tremor seems to pass through his whole frame, and then he turns over on his side dead, stretching out nearly sixty feet, with his flukes high above the water. All hands agreed that this was the gamiest whale they had ever killed. Any of the last three shots, the mate declared, would have killed a "new" whale, but when a whale, he said, was mortally wounded, he would die when he got ready, and you couldn't hurry him by shooting him again.

After the death of the whale the excitement rather increased than diminished. Down comes the captain from the masthead, and thick and fast gives his orders for securing the whale before he sinks. In this case, however, there was no occasion for hurry. It soon became evident that this whale would float; and after cutting off its flukes, to prevent resistance to the water, we soon had a cable round his tail and were steaming slowly home with the whale in tow. The whale had conducted us nearly ten miles off Race Point and the chase had lasted more than five hours. By five o'clock we had anchored the whale off the beach opposite the oil factory, where the blubber would soon be converted into some twenty barrels of oil.

Most whales sink as soon as they are dead, and rise to the surface again after three or four days, when they are secured by the whalers. The lances are marked with the whaler's initials so as to enable him to prove his property. It has recently been decided in the United States district court for the district of Massachusetts, in a very important case in which Provincetown and Wellfleet parties were interested, that these dead whales belong to the whalers who kill them, and not to the man who happens to tow them ashore. It was held that the killing of a whale with a bomb-lance was a sufficient appropriation of a wild animal (*feræ naturæ*) to constitute property. Had the decision of the court been otherwise, the whaling industry at the Cape would soon become extinct.

INDEX.

BLACKBIRD, cow, 39, 91, 98; crow, 17, 91, 101; red-shouldered, or red-winged, 18, 91, 101.
Bluebird, 11, 13, 32, 67, 80, 88, 92, 102.
Blue-jay, 87, 110.
Bobolink, 18, 67, 68, 69, 70, 79, 95, 97, 99, 103.
Bob-white, 106.
Bunting, bay-winged, 21, 83; towhee, 38, 85.

CATBIRD, 18, 42, 44, 45, 80, 98, 107.
Cedar-bird, 77.
Chebec, 53.
Cherry-bird, 77.
Chewink, 38, 39, 53, 72, 81, 85, 95, 101.
Chickadee, 15, 16, 42, 95.
Cow-bird, 39, 40, 41.
Crow, 50, 87, 106.
Cuckoo, 40, 67, 73, 91.

FINCH, grass, 21; purple, 18, 20, 24, 25, 26, 30, 50, 52, 59, 91, 98, 102.
Flicker, 17.
Flycatcher, least, 43, 53.

GOATSUCKERS, 62, 81.
Goldfinch, 18, 20, 27, 28, 50, 91, 98, 103.
Golden robin, 80, 85.
Grackle, blue, 17.
Greenlets, 52.
Grosbeak, blue, 57; cardinal, 57; rose-breasted, 55, 56, 97, 98, 101.
Ground robin, 38, 85.

HANGBIRD, 49.
Highhole, 17.
Huckleberry-bird, 84.
Humming-bird, ruby-throated, 54, 67, 72, 97, 101.

INDIGO-BIRD, 67, 71, 81, 88, 89, 98, 101.

www.ingramcontent.com/pod-product-compliance
Lightning Source LLC
Chambersburg PA
CBHW021937160426
43195CB00011B/1127